From Yale or Jail
How to
Get a Job

Kyler Frisbee

Cover art by Lindsay Minnich

LBMinnich Fine Art

DEDICATION

This Book is dedicated to each person who I have been blessed enough to know and learn from. I appreciate each of you. You believed in me when I didn't believe in myself.

CONTENTS

ACKNOWLEDGMENTS

Thank you to John and Mikala Collins for changing my life by the example you set. Thank you to my wonderful business partners and colleagues for continuing to progress and develop our industry. Thank you to Lee and Jane Scott and Pastor Judah and Chelsea Smith for leading me in my spiritual walk. Thank you to my wonderful family for the unconditional love and support that you have always given me. Thank you to my friends, for supporting me, laughing with me, and giving me the grace to grow. I love each one of you with all my hear

WELCOME

I am a member of the *NINJA* Generation, the generation that has been labeled: *No Income, No Job*, and no *A*ssets. No Way! We are not satisfied with this situation, and we will overcome the challenges before us. As our parents and grandparents retire, we will take up the reins of commerce and do what is right for our generation and future generations. We'll be financially literate, and we will ensure that our children have the opportunities that we ourselves have not. We are more than capable, more than ready, and we will not lead lives of quiet desperation. We are a creative, connected people, who believe in each other and what we can do together.

This book is meant to empower each of us with wisdom from multi-millionaires and elite professionals who have gone before us. This is for all of us who are ready to build, grow, and prosper. *NINJA* will mean *N*ew *I*ndustries, *N*ew *J*obs, and new *A*bilities. I feel completely comfortable saying to any reader, "These words will change your life!" They will open up a world of understanding and provide resources that you never knew existed. Your view of success will be more vivid, your life will be more vibrant, and your opportunities will be endless. I can stand behind these words because this information is not original. These words may be my own, but the concepts and lessons have been taught by thousands of people over the course of time. I take no credit for the content of this book. All of this information can be attributed to the thousands, perhaps even millions, of people throughout history who recognized their desire for more and chose to do something about it. I dare you to do the same.

This book is a well-rounded introductory approach to success, specifically: how to get the job. This is not meant to teach us how to succeed *IN* the jobs we want. It is meant to teach us how to *GET* them! This book is composed of ideas that have come from many of the most successful people throughout dozens of industries. These ideas come from executives and owners in Microsoft, Starbucks, Amazon, and many other companies that are thriving around the world. The intention of this book is to introduce each of us to important ideas as we begin the process of development. The key to success is a hunger to learn, to experience, and to contribute. This is not a book of magic moves that will grant us any job we wish for. However, if we apply the principles in these pages to our professional lives, we will separate ourselves from all other candidates time and time again. A race is not won with one great step; we will win the race one step at a time.

Now, over a dozen jobs in one decade may seem like a large number; and it is, I agree. I am a bit embarrassed to admit this, but just think of all the interviews, applications, and training programs I have gone through. Some changes were because of relocation, some were to gain new experience, but the biggest reason for job hopping is that I have been searching for the role I am meant to fill. I was and always will be searching for meaning and a chance to be great. Many of those positions had listed Bachelor's Degrees as must-haves to be considered. Even without a college degree, I was chosen over candidates who have had them. This is because of the lessons I am sharing with you. I am great at playing the game and I play to win. I have been offered great jobs, contributed to great companies and I am confident that you can also. Let us simplify the process, take the unknowns out of the equation, and prepare you to impress each of your future employers.

Each opportunity has given me a different view of myself, revealing to me which areas of my life needed to be refined and developed. I've acquired great training from many amazing people who have given me their insight, wisdom, and their "tricks of the trade." I have made great friends along the way, and I have been learning what makes companies great from all different perspectives. These topics I write about are areas in my life which have gone through great strain and improvement. Stretching myself in these areas has given me a deeper understanding and respect for myself. It has also given me an understanding of what employers, investors, and business partners are looking for.

Now, maybe you are reading this book with a hope that you will swiftly and smoothly embark on your career path, or perhaps you are looking to change directions in the journey called "success." Either way, I relate to you. There was a time when my family would ask me, "When are you getting a job?" And I have asked myself hundreds of times, "When am I going to begin my career?" In response to those questions I decided to actively and vigorously seek mentors and strategies to better my financial life and get on the path to success.

I now am blessed to be coached by three self-made multi-millionaires, in all walks of life. These men are virtuous gentlemen who have mentored me free of charge for nearly a decade to date. I have worked in retail, food service, and hospitality industries. I have been involved in the music industry, action sports, advertising, and I have owned multiple small businesses. I am now a business coach and recruiter for some of the most innovative companies in the Pacific Northwest.

The most important idea to understand is that doing the job and getting the job often require two completely different sets of skills. Time and time again candidates who aren't qualified are chosen over the candidates who are, simply because they know how to play the game and win. It has been said that the hardest part of the job is getting it. Now just like anything, there are strategies and skills that are necessary to be successful in an interview.

Mynor Alejandro Veliz, of Seattle, Washington, has one of the greatest stories of triumph and success and is currently the CFO of a large corporate solutions company. Mr. Veliz said, "There are many highly qualified people who have all the skills that are required and more, but they don't know how to play the (interview) game. At the same time there are people who lack certain required skills, but they are fantastic at playing the game and always get the jobs they interview for. For example, I chose a candidate who knew how to answer all my questions in a clear, concise, and direct way. Even though she had not used certain required skills in her previous jobs, she was able to give examples of how she had utilized those same skills in her personal life." This approach assured Mr. Veliz that this candidate had all the skills he was looking for, and more.

Many of us will read a list of qualifications for a position and believe that we will be disqualified if we don't fit perfectly. This may be true in industries like software engineering where a person has to have certain skills. However, there are usually many people who pass the "skill set" bar and between those people it's all about how they play the game. This is typically not the case for most other positions, as these lists are just starting points. The truth is that these qualifications just open the door, and if we can figure out another way to open the door then we will have the same shot as every other candidate. Most positions will not only require the skills to do the job, but they will require an ability to present these skills better than any other candidate.

Imagine…Waking up in the morning to find four offer letters from different companies in your inbox, asking you to meet with them to discuss your desired compensation. Meanwhile, you are getting two or three phone calls a week with new opportunities asking you to join them for an interview. Now your biggest concern is choosing the best company, compensation package, and ideal opportunity for you. Like this year's number one NFL draft pick, you will have companies and employers eager to persuade you to work for them. Now the choice is yours.

THE DRIVE

There are two great desires that drive the human spirit, the desire for love and the desire for purpose. This book is about the latter of the two. I believe most of us are more than qualified for the jobs we want, because I don't believe anyone wants to work a job they don't believe they can succeed in. Each of us will search for meaning and the roles that we are meant to fill. Once we've gotten these positions and we are up to speed, our employers will know that each of us was the right choice. The only thing that stands in our way is the interview process. What are companies looking for? What does it take to wow a prospective employer and be the most memorable candidate? How do we develop the confidence needed to express our qualifications clearly and prove that we are capable? Do we need to have a degree to get a good job?

There is much more to getting a job than being qualified to do the work. In order to be successful a person also needs to have a great attitude, a fantastic work ethic, and a vision of where they want to go. It has been said most hard-workers lack people skills and many likeable, caring, honest people lack a work ethic, but those who combine a great work ethic with fantastic people skills will make the greatest impact and lead the greatest lives. Over the years, I have acquired great knowledge and experience in impressing and connecting with employers, partners, and leaders. I have interviewed and have been coached by dozens of successful business owners, corporate executives, and elite professionals. These relationships were established through dedication, hard-work, and sheer perseverance. It is their insight and wisdom that fill these pages; I have simply been lucky enough to bring their words together. By understanding these concepts, each of us will be ready and able to beat out our competition and win the positions we are aiming for. I am a prime example of that.

I am asked constantly for advice by my peers in the area of networking, recruiting, and acquisition of high paying jobs. This is a collection of the notes I've taken and concepts I've learned. I write this book with a hope that it will have a significant impact in your life, and assist you in getting the job you want. I encourage you to explore the opportunities in this ever changing economic landscape and find opportunities that provide you with the type of life you want to live. Opportunities that inspire you to continue learning, push the envelope, and contribute, greatly, to society. Success is not a destination, it is a journey. The real reward is not what we receive from the journey, but who we become along the way. This book is meant to assist each of us in developing well rounded lives, full of satisfaction, joy, integrity, and character.

Imagine…What your dream life looks like…What would you be working on? Where would you be living? What would you drive? How would you spend your money? Who would you spend your time with? These questions should begin a process of creation. You create your life, because success is by choice; it is not by chance.

First we should start off by understanding the arena in which we are each playing in. Let's look at two hypothetical readers. Now the chosen field of one reader could be medicine or neuroscience. These fields require countless hours of dedication and sacrifice in which to become proficient. Hopefully the education, experience, and knowledge of this reader have prepared them to succeed in their field. The second reader is fresh out of high school hoping to begin their life of independence and the first step for them is to get a job, almost any job will do. The playing fields may be completely different, but the game plan to get the job is going to be the same. The principles in this book will prepare both readers to outshine their competition in their chosen field of endeavor. They may have been prepared differently with different capabilities, but the first obstacles are completely the same. It all starts with the first impression.

SECTION 1
PRESENTATION

APPEARANCE

Take the greatest chefs from any city in the world...Venice, New York, London, Paris...They all know the same thing. They may create the most exquisite delicacies the world has ever tasted. The feelings their guests experience will never be able to be expressed in words. Yet, they know that even if they create a culinary masterpiece, their work will not truly be appreciated if the dish isn't presented properly. Garnishes, placing, sauces, and even the extreme cleanliness of the plate itself, all prepare the guest to experience a delectable delicacy. Now if the world's greatest chefs concern themselves with details such as these, even though their creations have no equal, then shouldn't we be just as keen to present ourselves in a manner that prepares our employer to fully appreciate, and remember us?

I do not believe that it is a man's place to teach a woman how to be a woman. The topic of success, however, is not gender specific and these principles have worked for millions of women as well as millions of men. That being said, it is important to dress for the audience we are speaking with, for the role we want, and for the culture of the company that we are interviewing with. The first thing someone notices when we walk through the door is whether we take ourselves seriously. We communicate this by the clothes that we wear and how well we care for ourselves. Dress is directly tied to confidence; the better we dress the more confidence we exhibit and the more confident others will be in us. A well dressed person exudes confidence, feels better, stands taller, and says with their appearance, "I'm here. I belong here. Feel free to ask me why."

Today, dressing for success is not as simple as it once was.

Details in fashion are everything. A well-tailored one hundred dollar suit will look far more impressive than a four thousand dollar suit that has not been fit. The only advice I have for women, which is true for men also, is to remember that people should be more focused on what you're saying than what you're wearing (or not wearing), but you do want to fit in. Movies, magazines, and television are great places to begin researching fashion. Choose the styles you would like to wear from what people in your target industry are wearing. The more conservative look is going to be good for more traditional industries. I leave the flashy dressing to the athletes and celebrities, but there needs to be some balance between modern and classic. A suit is a great choice for the majority of interviews, however, when interviewing for the trades, it may be a little much. If that is the case, a pair of slacks, button up shirt, and a tie will be perfect. Remember that we are dressing to the culture of the company that we want to enter.

When stepping up your fashion repertoire, it is a good idea for men to begin their professional wardrobe with a dark navy suit. This, as opposed to black, is more versatile. The traditional black suit is typically more formal. Visit a clothing store for your measurements and be sure to find a salesperson with experience and knowledge. The general rule when building a quality wardrobe is to buy half as many items, but spend twice as much on each. Now in the beginning of your career if you require a larger wardrobe fast, it may be necessary to buy twice as many for half the price. I recommend doing extensive research into the items you are looking to purchase, and once you've built a satisfactory wardrobe, begin to upgrade piece by piece. Caring for your clothes properly will ensure that each piece will maintain a high quality for many years. Closely follow all instructions for washing your clothes properly.

Shoes are very important for both men and women. (However, most women already know this.) Most often the first things people look at on a man are his shoes and his watch. Remember the "half as many, twice as expensive," rule when purchasing shoes. If properly cared for, a good pair of shoes can last decades, sometimes a lifetime. With regular polish, cedar shoe trees, and the occasional resoling, you can be sure you will be placing your best foot forward time and time again. The polish will maintain the high quality and look of the leather. Shoe trees will pull the moisture after wearing and allow the shoe to maintain its shape and structure. Taking a pair of shoes to the cobbler every few years for a resoling will ensure that the leather stays tight and the sole is always strong and dry. Multiple pairs of shoes will also preserve the quality of each.

The rule with shoes and suits is that a person shouldn't wear the same suit or pair of shoes two days in a row, because these pieces need to air out and dry. After each wear, our suits should be hung neatly and shoe trees should be inserted. Our suits will need dry cleaning periodically. One timeless rule is that a suit coat should never be worn while driving. Most cars have a hook for clothes hangers on the ceiling next to the door. We can also hang our jackets on the back of our seats while we drive. Another rule of suiting up is that a man should never button the bottom button of his jacket. When men of the past carried swords as their weapon of choice, they had to be able to grab them quickly; this is why it is customary to leave the bottom button open on your jacket.

Be sure to buy high quality slacks as these will endure much activity throughout their lives. It is important to know how these slacks need to be washed. Also they should be neatly pressed and hung when not being worn. Socks should usually match the color of the pant leg or be basic black, but you can always spice up an outfit with a bright pair of socks. There are other basic guidelines for dressing when it comes to colors, patterns, and textures. These guidelines can be found by visiting your local clothier or by researching fashion articles online. Not only will you be greeted with more excitement than your less dressed colleagues, but like ZZ Top said, "Every Girl's Crazy 'Bout a Sharp Dressed Man!"

The most important theme to maintain in dress is that you are capable, clean, and up to date. Just like the culinary artists, you want your presentation to be inviting and enticing. Your appearance will spark interest and anticipation, and you will really dazzle them with what lies beneath the surface. Each of us has a brand, and we are marketing our brands to prospective companies and their clients. Branding is a multibillion dollar industry for a reason, how will you be remembered? What is your brand? These interviewers will be asking themselves and their colleagues, "Would we feel comfortable having this person represent us and our company to our clients and to the public?"

I would also recommend that you take this opportunity to explore casual attire as well. If your prospective employer were to see you out of his or her office after an interview, would they still remember you the same? Would your brand still be clean, capable, and up to date? You never know when you will meet the recruiting executive for your dream job or the CEO of an exciting start-up. I encourage you to take these concepts into your everyday life and begin to refine your everyday wardrobe as well.

For a serious lesson in fashion and more, every man should read the book, The Modern Gentleman by Phineas Mollod and Jason Tesauro. Also, for both men and women, a great forum for fashion examples is a new website/app called Pinterest. I encourage you all to explore both of these publications for examples and ideas in regards to fashion and more.

HEALTH AND HYGIENE

Now, as you can guess, what comes out of our mouths is going to be the most important aspect of an interview. That includes the appearance of our teeth and the scent of our breath. A friend of mine once described another person by saying, "His breath was kicking like Van Damme and Jet Li." If the smell of your breath knocks someone out like a UFC Fighter, you will be ineffective in communicating even your greatest qualifications.

Carry mints and gum as often as possible. Before an appointment, or after sitting though a presentation, we should assume that our breath needs some freshening up. This courteous act will be appreciated by all. The most important part of fresh breath is flossing. As food sits in our mouths it begins to break down. If left between our teeth over time it will become noticeable, I promise you. To ensure your words are received with a breath of fresh air, floss at least once a day before bed. Also, a proper brushing habit will ensure that our chompers are looking their best. It is important to schedule a cleaning with your dentist every six months to clean off the barnacles that have clung to your pearly whites. For people that would like to have teeth straightened or worked on, I would highly encourage you to do it as soon as possible. A smile is a fantastic tool in communication and you will need to be confident in your own for it to work effectively. Fresh breath is also attained and maintained by a fresh healthy diet, and constant hydration.

What we eat is directly affecting the scent of our breath, so consider eating healthy fresh meals for healthy fresh breath. A healthy diet affects more than simply our breath. When our body receives the fresh nutrients it needs it will operate at its highest level. You can be sure that your brain will function more clearly, providing you the heightened awareness that is needed to showcase your fantastic communication skills. You will get more done throughout your day as you eliminate the sluggish mid-day feelings.

Vitamins and supplements are more effective now than they have ever been. Still, research will show you what companies provide the best nutrition. It is important for us to research what types of supplements will be best for our individual situations. Supplements like Vitamin D3 are very important for people who live in places where the sun is not out constantly, because lack of sunlight can influence our moods and how our bodies function. Pro-biotics are important for healthy digestion and even a healthy complexion.

Maintaining a healthy complexion is a key element to confidence in my opinion. Each of us needs to be sure to wash our faces thoroughly with a good cleanser before bed and when we wake in the morning. Moisturizing will keep your skin healthy as you age. And washing or replacing your pillow cases every few days will keep your face looking young as if you slept on a cloud.

Exercise is a key factor in enhancing our abilities to think clearly and connect effectively. Your brain is cleansed and refreshed when your body is active. During exercise your heart rate increases, moving blood through your body faster providing nutrients and ridding the body of toxins. Your brain will be working more quickly as your synapses are cleansed and your neuro-pathways are cleared. This will ensure that you are able to communicate your thoughts and understand another's with ease. Exercise will also calm your nervous system as it rids your body of built up hormones. You will think more clearly and be emotionally stable with a consistent exercise habit. Your employer will be thrilled with your calm approach to challenges and your ability to handle conflict in a cool collected manner. Remember, stability and dependability are important to your prospective employers; show them that you can be their go-to person time and time again.

Be sure to choose a hairstyle that goes along with the wardrobe you are creating. Your hairstyle should be clean, crisp, and relatable. Visit a local stylist to find what would be the best for you. Again, it is important for us to know our audience, because what is accepted in one corporate environment may not be in another. Be sure that your eyes are easily seen as this is a large part of communication. When we look our best we showcase that we believe in ourselves. We feel capable and qualified. This will communicate to our future employers and clients that we are trustworthy, confident, and sophisticated.

These steps will take time to master and engaging in each of these steps at the same time may be overwhelming. Take your time and choose one or two of the these steps to begin with and go from there.

SECTION 2
MENTALITY

ATTITUDE

The most attractive attire is a great attitude and the most valuable accessory is a smile.

Now that you've impressed your interviewer with your impeccable appearance, the next character trait we'll examine is attitude. Do you believe in yourself? Do you believe in your skills? Do you believe that you are qualified? Do you believe in your worth? There's no doubt that the demand for quality employees is high, the question is; are you one of them? Your worth begins with the way you think. Do you see yourself as a problem solver, capable of independent thinking, or do you need others to make decisions for you? Are you accountable, and will you be able to be a student of the leaders in your new company? Do you have a desire to serve others and make a difference? Is it your intention to work with others for the betterment of the company? Or are you looking to be a part of a company so that others can work for you? The wealthy people in business are the ones that serve the most people the most effectively. Wealth is a measurement of the value that you have added to other peoples' lives. If you consistently serve and empower others, then money will follow you for life.

The most important part of showcasing your great qualities is that you must genuinely believe that you have them. Find what is good in everything, including you. Explore and record all of your great qualities. Start with your smile, laugh, unique creativity, and your care for others, and move on to all the other wonderful traits you have. The more worth you find in yourself, the more others will see in you. If you aren't happy now, you won't be happy when you are wealthy. We must love and respect ourselves before we can love and respect others. Do whatever you can to build confidence and love for yourself. Participate in activities that make you feel good about yourself.

Volunteering can give you an opportunity to contribute, network and develop new skills. Volunteering will also get you into the rhythm of working which will be noticeable to potential employers. Taking active classes like cooking or learning a new language will get us out of our comfort zones to meet new people. This will help you to appreciate your capacity for new experiences and get you back into the rhythm of learning. Engage in positive experiences that make you appreciate yourself with positive people who add value to you and build you up...and do the same for others. By taking our eyes off of ourselves, we will begin to understand how significant our impact on other peoples' lives can be.

There is a saying: input leads to thoughts, thoughts lead to action, action leads to habit, habit leads to character, and character determines whether we live a life of significance. This means that whatever we put into our brains will manifest in our actions and determine the outcome of our lives. If you have been inputting negativity into your brain, like I used to, then you will be giving life to that. Negative thoughts cannot simply be shaken off. They need to be diluted and starved before they turn themselves into negative actions. I have had to learn to starve the negativity that I had become accustomed to having in my brain and life. The habits that have been hurting me are being diluted by positive input. I read great books, listen to great lectures and talks, and I surround myself with incredible people who are focused on the beautiful parts of life. This is very important and has meant a great deal to my sanity and self-image.

SELF-IMAGE

Our self-image is the way we see ourselves and since we are the only ones who know what we do in private, our input and thoughts determine how we see ourselves; and how others will see us as well. I have learned not to get down on myself when I make mistakes. We must give ourselves grace to change knowing that we will not be perfect. We must continue to develop and refine ourselves; Rome wasn't built in a day.

Knowing this, Benjamin Franklin would focus on one character weakness and work on it for a full month, because change is not immediate and requires dedication and love for one's self. I've learned to understand myself and the moods I am in and now can pull myself out of mental slumps consistently. Thanks to Joe Rogan, Comedian and Sports Announcer, I have discovered and begun to explore sensory deprivation. These sessions place me in a pitch black tank of heavily salted water which is heated to my body temperature. This water allows me to feel like I'm a floating in space, forgetting about my body along with my other four senses. Once free from the chaos, my brain can completely engage in thorough exploration of all aspects of my life. These sessions heighten my awareness and provide clarity. In order to reset, I will also head to the gym to burn off some steam, put on some beautiful music, or get together with my favorite people to laugh and get out of the house. Find your reset button and use it often.

When I realize that I am dipping into an emotional slump the first activity I do is reconnect with nature. By a walking on the beach, hiking in the woods, or swimming in a lake, my spirit gets a fresh start. This is my way of refocusing on my humanity, and thus, part of earth and all around. Then I return to a clean car and clean home and I am ready to continue on my professional journey.

This is why a big part of cleansing my mental state is cleansing my personal space. I feel that when my home and car are in shambles my mental state is the same. It is easier to breathe and think in a clean space. I've met CEO's who have shared with me that the first thing they look at when they consider employing an executive is their car and their home. If these are not well kept, they assume the mental state is not either. A clean life often means a clean mentality. It is my responsibility to maintain stability in my emotions. Each of us must understand that we control our lives; both the quality and the outcome. Working is a great way to positively enhance both.

Develop a great work ethic and you will develop a great self-image. No one has ever accomplished anything great by asking, "How little can we do and still accomplish our goal?" That is because our self-images are directly connected to our work ethic. This is typically why most first generation multi-millionaires are more fulfilled with their wealth than those who have inherited theirs. Again, success is not the end result, but who we become along the way. We need to work hard enough to keep doubt from creeping in. If we haven't found a job yet we each can work at getting interviews and build our networks by serving other people. Staying busy will ensure that we don't sit and worry. It physically takes more energy and it is more draining to sit and worry than it is to work. Lazy people always have poor self-images and they are usually lazy because they don't believe they can contribute more. It can be a vicious cycle unless we know how to get out of it. If you get to work you will surprise yourself with what you are capable of. From this your self-image will grow and strengthen.

Most people do not suffer from a lack of intellect. They suffer from a lack of confidence and a low self-image. The most crippling symptom of a poor self-image is having a fear of people. The fear of the unknown often exposes itself in social settings. It is important to break down this fear little by little, by having conversations with strangers that push the limits. Our intention, at least for education's sake, should be to find out what is acceptable for us to say while in conversation with others. We shouldn't be afraid to offend someone a little bit if it is in an attempt to avoid the mundane. I have had many conversations that have surprised me because while I thought that I was crossing the line, my counterpart was enjoying the refreshing conversation and responded in delight. They appreciated that I wasn't afraid to talk about interesting topics, and by finding their boundaries we were able to talk about topics they didn't usually get to discuss.

Most people love an outgoing person who engages them in conversations that are out of the ordinary. Be different, be a breath of fresh air, become the best version of you, free from worry. Break down any superficial traits or habits that you've adopted and show the world the real you. People will admire and respect you for it, especially if you're a little weird. The only people who don't like outgoing people are the ones who are afraid of being outgoing themselves. We all must break out of our mundane routines and revitalize our spirits and our lives. When I moved in with a dear friend and business partner, I was the most uptight person you'd ever have met. I got overly offended by harmless jokes and I was easily embarrassed. My friend was a master at getting me out of my comfort zone. Through much embarrassment, we broke my shell and I learned to truly enjoy new experiences and new people; now, I thrive in all situations. I watched my friend push the limits with people by treating them as friends and being unafraid to really engage their spirit. I can't tell you how many times I've heard someone tell him, "I cannot believe that I am telling you this." Now, thanks to these experiences I can do the same thing.

My advice to you is say what you mean and mean what you say. Don't hold back in hopes of being polite, because often times it is more of an insult to leave something that needs to be said, unsaid. I have found that people really respect direct and honest statements and opinions. The characteristic that balances this element is having the ability to appreciate other people opinions, especially when they differ from our own. We need to eliminate the common expressions and small talk and ask engaging questions that are out of the ordinary. This will ensure that we are getting the most out of every conversation, and it will allow us to build friendships that are extraordinary

SERVANT-HOOD

Charles Schwab said that people skills are the highest paid skills in business. He said his smile alone was worth a million dollars. A great place to begin to understand and develop great people skills is in the book, "How to Win Friends and Influence People!" by Dale Carnegie. This will help you understand what you are doing that makes others love you and what you can do to help others love themselves. This is the second most sold book in history next to the Bible for a reason. Nearly all great men and women in all walks of life have read this book. It taught me that to be a great conversationalist, a person simply needs to be a great listener and ask questions. The number one topic people like to talk about is themselves and their favorite word is their own name. If you can learn to make people feel great about themselves they will love you for it. We each can make a major difference in each other's lives if we make a goal of being the first person to say someone's name. If you know someone's name, say it; it may be the only time they hear it that day or even that week.

I was told by my mentors that the most important work I will do in my life is that which I will not be paid for. It will be work that I do for other people and often it will cost me money to accomplish. I challenge you to become the best servant of others that your friends and family have ever known. Take this principle to your career and you will become the most sought after candidate in your industry. Each of us can be a catalyst for change; if we resolve to serve others in all areas of our lives, we will change the world.

Respect is perhaps the most misunderstood character trait in business. Respect is shown through servant-hood which communicates that we value another's time and convenience so much that we are willing to put it above our own. We communicate this through our speech and behavior. I've had to learn to eliminate profanity and complaints from my vocabulary. This is proper etiquette that ensures all people feel respected in conversation. I aim to provide a positive environment which allows others to focus their attention on matters at hand. I try to ask, "Is now a good time for us to talk?" "Can I get you anything?" "How can I make your life easier?"

In Japan, business is as much about manners as it is about profits. I've learned to remember names, be early to appointments, and be quick to return calls, texts and emails. I choose to inconvenience myself to serve and show my appreciation for others. I have become others focused with a servants heart…this has been one of the most rewarding lesson I've learned in life.

SUCCESS PRINCIPLES

A deep understanding of the success principles, which have yielded tremendous results throughout history, will be the building blocks to any empire we hope to construct. These lessons will come from all areas of life and all corners of the globe. Regardless of whether we ask an athlete such as Michael Jordan, an entertainer like Will Smith, or President Abraham Lincoln, the lessons they would share with us would be surprisingly alike. This is because success in any endeavor requires the same resilience and determination, along with a vast understanding of dozens of other concepts.

The most important lessons I have learned are not about how to play the interview game. They are the skills I have gained from diverse opportunities. These ideas and principles now govern my entire life. I have learned to fail forward and pick myself up knowing that I am still moving in the right direction. This is a phenomenal accomplishment in itself.

Michael Jordan said he missed more game winning shots than he ever made, Wayne Gretzky said that he missed more shots on the net than he ever scored, and Thomas Edison failed over ten thousand times while creating the light bulb. The only comment Edison made when asked why he kept going was that he had simply found ten thousand ways that his invention would not work. That was vital to his accomplishment. His mentality *allowed* each failure to be a success.

In searching for the right job it is vital that we do not allow failures to keep us from succeeding. If we are turned down by a prospective employer, it is important that we continue to seek the best opportunities and learn from the experiences we've had.

Consider asking an interviewer who chose another candidate what you could have done better. Ask them what they liked about you and what characteristics they would have preferred that you had. This may be a little embarrassing or nerve-racking, but it will be far more helpful than harmful to your growth and future success. If you explain to them the reason you are interested in learning their opinion, surely they will be more than happy to explain! If we approach them with an attitude of disappointment, anger, or criticism we will simply be encouraging them to defend their decision and justify themselves, which will *not* be beneficial to our overarching purpose.

While speaking with two recruiters who work with employers and people in Bellevue, Washington, I was not surprised to hear their biggest complaints about job seekers were regarding their attitudes. These women said that job seekers are often short with them and rude to them without ever expressing appreciation for their assistance. These professional recruiters told me that they will not even entertain the idea of sending one of these people to their clients for interviews. These job seekers did not understand the fundamental golden rule, which is treating others as you would like to be treated. It is important to approach all people, especially those helping you, with an attitude of appreciation and humility-the type of humility that allows you to tell another how important their work is and how much it means to you. These recruiters also told me that their clients, some of the most prestigious companies in the world, understand one thing; a person cannot simply change the amount of experience they have had in a field overnight. They can, however, control their attitude and the manner in which they treat other people. These companies also said that they would take positive people skills over qualified experience any day.

THE WARRIOR AND THE KING

I was told a story about a Warrior and a King. A soldier back from a long journey, after losing many of his comrades to the enemy and the elements, requested an audience with the King. The soldier was enraged by the orders that left his dearest friends to be buried by the falling snow. Clutching his sword he made his way to the Grand Hall for his meeting with the King. As he approached the ancient doors, the Queen exited the Hall. With a woman's intuition she examined the lonely soldier. She stopped him, kissed his hand and wept upon his sleeve. The soldier realized in the pain of loss, he was not alone. He released his sword and removed his helmet as he entered the Hall of the King. He found the King upon the throne, but his crown had fallen to the floor, and his robes were soaked with tears. When he saw the face of the lonely soldier the King fell to the ground to mourn. Our humble King asked for forgiveness and explained his error in judgment. Our soldier learned a great lesson that day for he had prepared for a duel with a Warrior, but was humbled in meeting his King.

When we approach a leader in conflict, we will either be searching for understanding or seeking to criticize their judgment. In doing so, we will either be speaking to the Warrior or the King. When approaching this leader with a humble spirit we will be speaking to the noble King. He will be the understanding, collected, and empathetic leader who cares for his people and acts in their best interest. He will outstretch his hand and his wisdom to anyone who seeks it, and he will be a man who desires to serve. However, if we approach the same leader with an attitude of criticism, resentment, or condemnation we will undoubtedly be speaking to the Warrior. With his hand on his sword and the other clutching his shield, he will defend himself and his actions against any attack, because our great King is also a great Warrior. He will block all attacks and strike swiftly with the strength of the ages and without compassion he will leave all opposition defeated in his wake. If defeated, he will fight until he cannot any longer, with all the heart a true Warrior possesses. So we must be aware of the spirit in which we approach our leaders and other persons of authority, because this will determine whether we dine in the Royal Hall or enter the Coliseum as a Gladiator.

THE POWER OF PERCEPTION

Perception has a great deal to do with the way people will interact with us and the way we interact with others. The King's perception of us must be one that resembles a manner of humble submission in order for him to be the gracious King we need. Perception is all about the way a person sees a situation. This is why we started this book with a chapter on appearance. The initial introduction, or perception, will dictate a person's view of you from that moment on. It is vital that we maintain positive perceptions of others in our daily lives. This will ensure that we are able to have positive attitudes as we interact with strangers, colleagues, and even our closest relationships.

This book is about becoming a well-rounded person in order to become a well rounded employee, executive, and partner, we need to touch on a point that if not addressed can cause a great deal of harm. Have you ever had a colleague or acquaintance you didn't know very well, but you had a perception of them as being friendly, genuine, and pleasant? Yet a friend you had became frustrated and said something less than pleasant about your colleague. Now, your perception of your colleague will usually change regardless of whether your friend's statements were accurate or not. This is why gossip is so dangerous and can legally be seen in business as slander.

Now, think back, have you ever said something about another person out of frustration or anger? This statement probably altered the way the person you were speaking with viewed the person you were speaking about. Now more importantly and even less obvious, these statements have altered the way you now see the person of whom you are speaking. So if we are talking bad about a friend behind their back, we will feel awkward and fake the next time we see them. It is important that we learn to bridle our tongue when our emotions heat up. This is because the power of the spoken word affects our spirits and mentalities far more that most of us realize.

THE POWER OF THOUGHT
AND SPOKEN WORD

Self-talk is the most important part of building a self-image. A great man once told me that we should not pay any attention to criticism or compliments, for we do not completely know the life of that person or the motives behind their statements. Let no man persuade you to think a certain way about yourself. The most important part of building self confidence is recognizing all of our great attributes and accepting all that we need to work on. This sounds very self-focused, because it is. In the same way servant-hood is completely about other people, self-image and self-talk are all about each of us, personally. Your self-talk is made up of mantras, thoughts, and words that encourage you to be the person you want to be. They must assure you that you are a person worthy of all you want.

If we are not to listen to the comments of others, then it is left up to each of us to develop confidence and belief in ourselves. The fact is, each of us has habits that we wish we didn't and habits that we want to create. Each time we do something that we desire not to, we hurt our self-image and confidence. Every time we do what we believe is best for ourselves we strengthen our belief in ourselves. Integrity is doing the right thing even when no one else can see, so behind closed doors we are either building ourselves up or breaking ourselves down.

As a kid playing too many video games and longing to have real friends, it was up to me to turn off the games and step out of my house. I made the decision to join clubs and teams and projects in hopes of building real relationships and my confidence soared when my desires came to fruition. I encourage each of us to think about everything that we love about ourselves. We must reassure ourselves daily that we are amazing people, capable of anything. We must envision the goals we want to achieve, because on our journey toward becoming the best we can be, each of us sets our own course and speed.

The power of the spoken word has been mentioned in books like "The Secret," "Psycho Cybernetics", and even long before Christ in the Old Testament of the Bible. For more information on this topic, more research will be greatly beneficial. The power of the spoken word concept states that whatever we speak and think, we become. If input leads to thoughts and thoughts lead to speech and speech leads to action, then what we listen to, read, and watch will determine what we think, speak, and do. If we input positive information (books, talks, and music) we will speak affirmations, and then we will become what we want to become.

It is so important for us to compliment ourselves and reaffirm that we are what we want to be. If a person has trouble being organized, it is a great idea for them to reaffirm in their thoughts and with their statements that "I am organized." One of my first affirmations that I repeated whenever I was nervous, was "I am a healthy, happy, confident, Christian, billionaire." These affirmations helped dictate the way that I thought about myself. Now in the beginning it felt almost impossible to control my thoughts, so I turned it into a game. If I ever realized that I was thinking negatively about myself or judgmental thoughts about another person, then I recited my affirmation in my head.

My affirmations have changed over the years, dozens of times, because once I became what I was thinking about, I moved on to other areas which I wanted to change and develop. Some of the affirmations only involved me, and others involved the people around me. I had to learn to appreciate others and love all people in order to truly be happy. So one of my affirmations was, "I am love (and I would feel the words that I was thinking), you are love (and I would then focus my attention on others)." The power of this affirmation changed and dictated my perception of other people, which was one of the most important and beneficial changes I have undergone. Today I absolutely love people, and I often think to myself, "I can do all things through Christ who strengthens me." Another impactful mantra has been, "I am, you are, I accept." This affirmation has produced the most recent change in my life. It has been powerful in eliminating the judgment and criticism of others. When I think, "I am," I take a moment to fully appreciate myself and where I am and what I am doing. When I think, "you are," I take a moment to appreciate all the people around me and often think of all the people in the world as if we are all connected. I don't analyze people, I just observe. Then I finish my thought with, "I accept," which has taught me how to accept myself and others without judgment or criticism. This has been a wonderful practice that has yielded great results, and I encourage everyone to use it.

This is the first time I have really told anyone about the practice that goes on in my thoughts. I have chosen to dictate my thoughts, rather than letting random thoughts dictate the type of person I become. This brings me to the next success principle I have learned.

SUCCESS IS NOT BY CHANCE, IT IS BY CHOICE

Henry Ford said, "Whether you think you can or think you can't, you are correct." Everyday people ask themselves, "Why aren't I further along in my career?" "Why do those people have such great lives and so much, when I have so little?" "How have those people been so successful, what is it that I don't know?"

The statement I believe to be spoken most is, "I wish…" Instead of wishing, the people who succeed make the decision to get where they want to be. This decision is not just a snap decision that is made once only in thought. There is a saying, "Three frogs are on a log, one decides to jump off. How many frogs are left? Three, just because he made the decision does not mean he followed through." So the decisions that successful people have made have also been followed with action. They developed plans, executed ideas, and they decided to sacrifice all the comforts of the good life for the great life. These decisions are made time and time again because once we execute one plan we have to create the next.

By practicing the principles in the book, the Slight Edge by Jeff Olson, we will establish the lives we want to live. The book the Slight Edge is about an incredible concept that teaches us how important it is to make the right decisions every day. An example Mr. Olson uses is that making poor food choices today will not kill us, but making that same decision every day will have some negative consequences to our health. In turn, making the decision to eat right and exercise today may not give us the health or physique that we desire, but that same decision made every day will develop a beautiful body inside and out. Success in any endeavor is not about being at the right place at the right time, it is about making sure that we are prepared when we are at the right place at the right time. We will not succeed by chance, but by choice.

I am the captain of my own ship and so are you. Being strong willed is not about an over-bearing presence. It is about deciding on a goal, making a plan, and following through to the realization of that goal. No one else can push us or pull us to success. That is a journey that each of us must take on our own. Along the way, we will have people with whom to walk; people who will assist us, and even some who will reveal new paths for us to explore. We will also do the same for others, but the most important part of our journey is that each of us sets our OWN course, individually.

Each of us has a vision of where we want to go, so pack up and set course. Whether we encounter storms, icebergs, or tidal waves, we are each the captain of our own ship and will decide how to proceed. Do we charge through the challenges, do we turn back for shore, or do we abandon ship? The beauty of the journey is that when each of us gets to the destination we envisioned, we each will know that we chose it for ourselves. We will each personally choose, consciously or subconsciously, the lives we live. The subconscious choices will be based on the ideas we are inputting into our brains. The point is that, when we get to where we want to be, we each will know that the place we made it to was specifically chosen for us, by us. Then we can plot a chart for our next adventure. These charts for our future are also known as dreams or visions.

VISIONS AND GOALS

Goals and dreams are our intellectual property, blueprints for our lives. They are not for others to take or change.

Most people believe that telling our friends our goals will keep us accountable to them. Psychologists say that this is actually untrue. It will actually give us the feelings that we have already achieved our goal. Our mind will often mistake the talking for actually doing. I can't tell you how many times I've told someone that I'm writing a book, become all excited about it by talking to them, and then looked back a week later and realized I hadn't typed a word. So in order to build an action plan and a path to success, we must consult first with ourselves. If we can convince ourselves that we are going to accomplish our goals, then no one else's opinion matters. There is a saying that goes like this, "The more we love our decisions, the less we need others to love them."

The only times I really seek another person's opinion or encouragement is when I doubt my own abilities. I only go to a select group of people who have proven that they want the best for me and have my best interest at heart. It is not worth risking the onslaught of negativity or discouragement from naysayers or the "I told you so," in the event that I fail. There is glory in failure if we whole heartedly try again, because failure is not final. Success is not clean; it is messy, chaotic, and full of failures and victories. We all need some encouragement along the way. We each must find people who will support and encourage us. Be sure to avoid people who may try to steal your dreams.

One of the most important ingredients for success is a well-defined vision for our lives. In order to find the best opportunity for our lives it is imperative that we have an ideal life envisioned.

When we set out on our journey we must have a direction. Henry Ford, founder of the Ford Motor Co., said this, "You don't have to see the entire staircase; you just need to see the next step." We don't necessarily need to know exactly where we want to go, but we do need a direction along with the will to take another step. Once we choose the direction we want to travel in our careers, we must choose which road we want to travel down. There are many ways to get to our next destination.

College can be a great stepping stone; however, those that decide not to attend college can gain experience through jobs they choose along the way. We must not get caught up in thinking there is only one way to get the opportunities which we want. My goal has been to be in the financial industry since I was a kid. I didn't go the traditional route of a college degree, internship, and financial professional. My route, after leaving school unfinished, was going from management to sales, and into the retail banking industry and then into the financial field. Now, I have chosen to serve others on their way to their professional dreams. Along the way I have founded three companies, two of which are still growing and have extremely bright futures. All of these jobs and business ventures have taught me real world lessons that I have applied to my career, my companies, and my personal relationships. School was not the right direction for me because I was not able to focus in a classroom and I was not mature enough to understand the benefits at the time. I needed to experience and learn through action in live situations.

Each one of us has more access to self-education than anyone in history. We have opportunities to explore industries, events, and world affairs in a way that would have been far beyond our reach in prior generations. We have the ability to study innovation and learn more about the industries we're interested in. By learning about other industries we can understand how our career choices fit into the big picture and global economy. We may even find fields that interest us more than the ones we had chosen to explore. We must be open to learning and open to new opportunities. Free online courses are available to introduce us to different lifestyles and subjects.

By keeping up with current events, we prove that we are

aware of the lives outside of our own. I encourage each of you to learn about international affairs starting with the way governments and companies around the globe work together. Many jobs are being outsourced to foreign countries due to the financial advantages and the fact that India and China are graduating more English speaking individuals every year than any other county, (including America.) We must pay attention to these changes and learn which industries will be affected.

Once we decide on a route and embark on our endeavor, we must be determined to be the best we can at whatever we do. We need to set goals, short term and long term. Even if we give it a go and miss the mark, we will be moving in the right direction. We cannot allow our current situations to get us down if they are not what we want. Your life now is a result of the past decisions you've made and not a result of who you are today. Each of us will need to begin to make better and healthier decisions that will put us where we want to be in the future.

Learn to disconnect yourself a bit from your current situation. Try looking at your life from a different perspective. Work on developing areas that are weak, and build up areas that are strongest. Remember, each of us will usually be our own harshest critic. It is very difficult to see the changes and progress we make personally from the inside. As you begin your journey of success, people will notice, some will criticize you and others will cheer you on. Either way, accept it as a sign that you are growing. Always assume that you've grown way more than you think you have. Don't worry about anything down the road, just work on one step at a time. Please understand that this transition and process will take time. Don't be afraid of going slow, be afraid of standing still. Memories of past failure or pain cannot harm us if we are focused on future success and endeavors.

In order to choose what the best route is for our lives, it is a good idea to determine the way we want to live. We need to find an opportunity that provides the lifestyle we want, not just the activity we want to perform. We need to ask ourselves, "How much time am I willing to put into my career?" "How much travel will I be comfortable with?" Weigh these against your other goals like having a great marriage and spending time with your loved ones.

Perhaps you dream of being a fulltime parent or spouse by developing a great residual income. Perhaps you want to be the best in an industry through considerable work and extreme dedication. Determine how you want to live and what you are willing to give up in order to be living that way. Life is not about making money, but business is, and money is a necessary tool for most of our lives. Our careers will be very important parts of our lives, but I don't believe they will be or should be the largest parts of our lives. That being said, I do believe strongly in hard work and dedication, but I equally believe that a passionate marriage and great relationships will be the most rewarding "investments" any of us will ever make.

Before you have a job it is important to determine what you are willing to do in order to succeed. Are you willing to close deals that may hurt other people if they profit you and your company? Are you willing to lie, cheat, or steal to make it to the top? Are you interested in doing anything, even if it breaks God's laws or man's laws, in order to be the best? Do you want to be doing things for the greater good and betterment of others? If you develop a sound moral code prior to employment, you will have established a moral compass that if you live by it, will ensure you stay on the path you desire to journey down. It is a dangerous place to have to decide what you are comfortable with right in the middle of a controversial situation. More structure in your plan prior to beginning your job search will provide you with a plotted course and a game plan to run with. True, much in your life may change as opportunities present themselves, but it has been said, "If you aim for nothing you will hit it." So be sure to have a plan and a vision for your future.

As we think about our moral code, we need to think about what types of contributions we would like to make in others' lives. What needs in peoples' lives are we interested in filling? In what areas of their lives are we interested in assisting them? If you can combine a passion you have, with an area in other peoples' lives that need attention, then you will be successful. What areas of your life are you interested in bettering? For me, relationships and finances have always been a passion. I am intrigued by what makes great relationships and how great people skills are developed. I am also interested in the accumulation of wealth, how it can be preserved and used, and the opportunities that it presents. I have also been very interested in how people work together to move money around in order to get things done. Even the most compassionate and humanitarian ideas and non-profit companies need money to gain their footing. Impact investors are asked to negotiate worthwhile investments that yield desirable returns and provide resources for life changing ventures to grow. I am interested in how this works, what makes a business a worthy investment, and what makes a businessman a worthy partner. This passion has brought me to a point in my life where it is an honor to share the information I have attained. This is ultimately a book of what makes a person a credible, trustworthy partner in business and in employment. Success starts in the heart, finding exactly what you want personally then developing that passion and using it to better others' lives as well as our own.

VOCABULARY AND COMMUNICATION

Now we are on to the topic of communication, which is the art and skill that allows us to share ideas. This lost art was once so elegant that even the driest dialogue of America's founding fathers, to us today, seems to have been written by Shakespeare. It has been said by great men and women that lack of communication is death in any relationship. Now if that is true then we can say that conversation is a vital part of a relationship's survival and better communication will lead to stronger relationships. This art will be our means for expressing our ideas, desires, and qualifications for the jobs we want. We will separate ourselves from our competition once again in the way we speak and how well we articulate our desires and ideas for the future.

Now as beautiful as America's founding fathers spoke, today their words cannot hold the same clarity or function. I encourage you to strive for efficient communication over intellectual, and even over beautiful dialogue. By this I mean, strive to be understood clearly and if extravagant words will communicate your message more clearly, use them. If these words interfere with the clarity of your message then your message will be confusing and be misunderstood. Instead of using energy to sound smart and elegant, perhaps we can use it to ensure our messages are being clearly understood. Words don't only carry meaning, they also carry feelings. So word choice actually dictates how our partners in conversation feel.

Often, days after a conversation, our audience/counterpart will not remember the words that were spoken. When they recall the interaction they will remember the way that we made them feel. Much more is communicated than simply a message. Consider the way you make a person feel while with them because feelings are more memorable than words. Feelings are like a thermometer, they simply measure how we interpret a situation. In my opinion words and the way we say them are the thermostat and thus dictate the way people will perceive our messages. The greatest communicators have been able to deliver any message, regardless of the nature, in a manner that is pleasantly received.

Before I understood the importance of a well versed vocabulary, my conversations often consisted of the same words to describe very different situations. The most common word I used was awesome. I would say to my friends, "That meteor shower was awesome...That Castle was awesome...Even that donut was awesome. The level of my enthusiasm was never expressed appropriately because the description of each situation was not expressed any differently. Imagine, being an interviewer and asking your candidate, "How was your last job?" "It was good," they respond. You follow up by asking, "Can you elaborate, please?" Then they say, "The Company was good, my co-workers were good, and the office supplies were good." Do their answers give you any reason to believe they will be able to communicate a message effectively or even comprehensibly? Now consider another candidate saying, "My old boss was a thrilling leader, he was able to connect with his team in a manner that provided clear instruction and outlined the benefits." Who would you choose to represent you and your company to your clients and employees?

Mastering the art of communication should be a lifelong pursuit. Few activities in life will benefit you more than expanding your vocabulary. Having an extensive vocabulary will allow you to connect with people in many different industries. Each industry has its own caveat of industry-specific words that professionals in those fields use frequently. For a person interested in working in the financial field it will be greatly beneficial to understand the difference between APR (Annual Percentage Rate...what you pay the bank on a loan) and APY (Annual Percentage Yield...what the bank pays you on an investment or deposit.) If we want to work in the fashion industry we will need to know what a hemline and patterns are. For the automotive industry we may need to know what a differential is. Knowing a fair amount of industry specific words will help us to connect with many more people in our everyday life. It will also protect us from being taken advantage of by unethical people when we look for advice and service. However, these words are like tools that are meant for a specific purpose. It is important to know when to use them and when they are not necessary.

When I began the process of expanding my vocabulary and ability to speak, the greatest activity for me was and still is reading out loud. By reading other peoples words I was able to hear them being spoken and practice the annunciation of these well thought out sentences. This enabled me to use these words in my daily life, broadening my vocabulary and giving me confidence as I learned to speak well. It is a powerful thing to hear ourselves speak the words of history's most talented authors. When we speak like successful people we also begin to think like them. I have known many people who became bolder in conversation and even defeated speech impediments by reading out loud. In an age of emails, texts, and excessive slang, reading out loud taught me to speak in complete sentences and communicate my ideas effectively. This has been one of the greatest and most utilized skills in my day to day life.

FINANCES

Life is not about making money, but business is. Before you even develop your income, it is important to have a plan for what you will do with it. Financial literacy is not taught as thoroughly as it should be in most of our education system. This is the cause for ridiculous credit card balances, a huge foreclosure rate, and bankruptcy now being a "smart financial decision." One of my mentors told me that when he was starting his first pharmacy, he bounced a check by accident. He went to the bank to straighten it out, with the expectation of being handcuffed and arrested. Now, it is vital that we understand interest rates and what it means to finance our everyday purchases.

I was told that if I am financing pizza and underwear I have some serious financial problems. You might say, "I'd never finance pizza…" Well thousands, maybe millions, of people put these types of purchases on their credit cards and they are unable to pay off the balance at the end of the month. This means they've financed their pizza and any other everyday items they've purchased. If you can't pay off your credit card at the end of the month, you had better start listening to people who do. Why take advice from people who do not have lives that you want to live? So, chose to follow people who have financial statements and lifestyles that you dream of. I'm not a billionaire yet, but I know some people who are incredibly wealthy and these lessons come from them. I'm just the messenger.

Now to fully understand finances each of us will need to do our own research, ask our own questions, and find our own mentors. This is just a basic starting point to give us a foundation to build on. Financial stability begins with a budget. Companies build balance sheets which show their income vs. expenses and this is what each of us should be doing as well. I was told that to be truly financially successful it is vital that I run my life and home with the same standards of a multimillion dollar corporation. An effective budget begins with adding up monthly income, then subtracting the fixed expenses like car notes, savings, cell bill, rent or mortgage, and insurance. Then subtract the variable expenses that may change from month to month, like a grocery budget, a gas budget, and so forth. Then if there are extra funds remaining, this is what we call discretionary funds. This means you get to spend these funds at your discretion on things like entertainment and other non-vital purchases. I would encourage each person to deposit a healthy amount of discretionary funds into a savings account. Before we begin to indulge in luxuries, it is wise to save up at least 6 months of living expenses in a savings account, just in case we lose our jobs or experience unforeseen emergencies. Most multi-millionaires build their wealth on great budgeting and savings.

My mentors have built extremely healthy residual income streams, but they've been able to build great wealth by utilizing these principles responsibly. I suggest reading the book, "The Millionaire Next Door," to understand the principles of living below your means. If your expenses are larger than your income after taxes you have a decision to make. You can either trim the fat by lowering your car note, finding a new home or bringing in a roommate; or you can decide to make more money. If your job is not providing a large enough income you may need to get another job or find odd jobs to make more money. The most intelligent and stable form of secondary income that I've seen has come from starting a network marketing business. Robert Kiyosaki, author of Rich Dad Poor Dad, calls network marketing The Business of the 21st Century in his book with the same title. Some other ways of creating a residual income can be investing in the stock market or real estate ventures, but these often require a large capital to invest with no guarantee that they will pay off, but we will touch more on diversification later.

The number one cause for financial distress is the overuse of debt. It has become very easy for young people to obtain credit cards and loans without any education about how to use them.

Warren Buffet said on a youtube.com interview, "If you are smart you don't need to use debt and if you're dumb you have no business using it." It is my goal to avoid living a fake lifestyle. I don't want to be a person who buys things I don't need to impress people I don't know and who probably don't care. Why finance a car I can't afford just to have people say, "Wow, that's a nice car!" Is this really worth putting my whole financial future in jeopardy? It is much more difficult to get out of debt than it is to get in it. If we neglect to understand the consequences we may live in debt for our entire lives. Sometimes financing portions of a purchase is an intelligent decision, but be sure to understand who you are taking your financial advice from.

Though most bankers and financial advisors aim to serve, they still have goals and quotas to meet and this will undoubtedly affect their counsel. Find people who have the financial statements you want to obtain and listen to them. Great people to start with are financial guru's Robert Kiyosaki, Dave Ramsey, Warren Buffett and they are just the beginning. Robert Kiyosaki is one of the most read financial authors of our time. He has educated millions on the importance of building assets to generate wealth. His book Rich Dad Poor Dad is a great foundation for financial literacy. Dave Ramsey is a budgeting master whose messages and lessons make financial literacy easy to understand. Warren Buffett, billionaire owner of Berkshire Hathaway, is a great person to listen to if you are searching to understand what makes the ultra wealthy, wealthy. His talks often credit his great success to common sense and integrity, not simply savvy business decisions.

The overall picture and idea is for each of us to be aware of the life want to live in the future. It will be our lives that we are building or sacrificing every day, and it will be our decisions that will determine what resources will be available in the years ahead. A question we need to ask ourselves is whether our next purchase is more important than our future goals. If my goal is to pay cash for a car or home then I should be completely happy to eliminate eating out, cable TV and a new pair of shoes because these small purchases add up over time.

Each of us can contribute to a generation and global economy that are more financially responsible and less inclined to follow the seduction of the latest trend. I agree that we cannot neglect our present lives in order to build a great future, because there is no guarantee that we will be here tomorrow and we can't take the wealth with us. The choices we make will determine the balance in our lives between the pleasures of today and the options of tomorrow. If we choose to be diligent in our decisions and build solid financial futures, we can make a difference in the history of the world and be remembered as the Next Great Generation. What will we leave for those coming next, what will we cultivate for our tomorrows, and what will truly make us happy today?

CREDIT

As a financial consultant for many people I've learned that it is not always possible to pay cash for the things we need and want, like houses and cars. In order to make these types of major purchases most of us will request a loan from our chosen bank or credit union. These financial institutions base their decisions to lend mostly on our current income and our credit scores. These two numbers play the largest part in assuring a bank that we will pay back our loans. The decisions we make in our early twenties and thirties have significant impact on our future options. Every one of us starts out with a perfect credit score. As we use credit cards from our banks or our favorite stores, our credit either stays perfect at an 850 or it begins to go down. In order to build credit we need to start slow and small in ways that we are sure we can pay back.

What I've learned from working in some great financial institutions is that there are very responsible ways to use lines of credit and loans. A credit card is the most common form of a line of credit. This means a lender will allow us to use their funds at the present moment and in return we will pay them back. They know that most of us will over spend and not be able to pay off all of the balance at the end of every month. This is how lenders make their money. Interest begins to build the first day of the month if we don't pay off the balance from the month before. These cards have huge interest rates and it is not unheard of for amateur users to pay back double the amount they spent. Sometimes people will spend the total amount that a card will allow and can only afford to pay off the interest the balance accrues every month. If they continue this behavior they will never, in their entire lives, pay off the balance of the card.

So, if we are going to be intelligent about the way we borrow and preserve our options of using credit to purchase houses, cars, and education, we need to pay back every dollar we spend and do so every month. There are some great benefits to using credit cards responsibly. Many of these credit cards will earn the user rewards on dollars spent. These will often add up to airline tickets, cash back, or other incentives. These credit card companies want to persuade us to use their cards, so they offer us great rewards. The key for us, not the lenders, is to pay off the cards every single month. Credit scores affect more than just our ability to borrow money. Extremely low credit scores can often disqualify candidates from jobs, whether it is in finances, insurance, or even basic sales companies. So we must be sure to use our options wisely and never fall to the temptation of overspending. This will ensure that we are a generation of change, integrity, and financial responsibility.

CURRENT EVENTS

At some point you will have to ask yourself, "How involved in this world do I want to be?" "Would you be satisfied living far off the grid in the mountains, skiing, snowboarding, fishing, and hiking? Or would you be more fulfilled in a big city working in a high rise amassing millions and building an empire?" The answers to these questions will guide you to the greatest life you could imagine. I have balanced my love for enterprise with my love for the great outdoors, but there are no greater causes for my life than to be a faithful Christian, wonderful husband, honorable father, and to lay down my life for my friends. I learned that part of being a great husband and father means being a great provider and a great example.

In order to be a great friend and colleague you must be aware of the current state of the world including the individual countries within it. You must understand the relationships between industries, past, present, and future. You must understand the common goals and vision for the future along with the challenges we will face together. Thus, always be reading, listening, and learning about what is happening in your country and around the world. What are the daily changes that will affect the way your children grow up and live? What are the changes that are going to affect the way that your parents spend their golden years? How will these changes impact your family as you build your lives and what can you do to make a difference?

Current events are not simply the latest act on the stage of life. These events often will determine our way of life for decades and centuries to come. It will be vital, to our survival and prosperity, to understand how global empires work together or in conflict, because our national economy rolls with the tide. It is important to understand local and national legislation before it is voted on, because we do not want to wake up one morning to find that our freedoms have been stripped away. We must not let anyone strip them away little by little, because that's how you boil a frog.

You can't boil a frog by throwing him in a boiling pot of water, he will jump out. However, if you place him in the water and turn the heat up little by little, the frog will stay put even until he boils to death. Now that is a gruesome illustration, but it is effective in communicating this point. Don't be the frog that isn't paying attention to his surrounding and ends up boiling to death. I am engaged in learning about the decisions that have led us to where we are today. History books have taught me the good, the bad, and the ugly regarding the choices leaders have made and what circumstances and perspectives led to those decisions. It is my intention to make great decisions for my family, contribute to great decisions for my companies, and instill this understanding in the generation we will raise.

Current Events are more important than we realize. Not only will we be able to carry on conversations with colleagues and clients about the latest changes and challenges, but we will understand what led us to where we are, along with some effective strategies to move forward. In any industry it will be vital for us to know our surroundings and the impact these changes are leaving. Developing understanding and awareness allows us to deepen our connections and strengthen the bond between ourselves, our communities, and the rest or humanity. We must understand, we must be aware, and we must develop opinions and ideas, because we will have more of an impact on this world and the future than any one of us can realize.

MENTORSHIP

The only reason I am able to write this book is because of the priceless wisdom that has been cast down to me from men and women who have gone before me. They have developed lives that I want and they are selfless people who understand that their contributions into my life will spider web and spread impacting thousands, and eventually millions, of lives. I have chosen a life of learning...from real life multi-millionaires, passionate husbands and wives, and community leaders. These men and women have instilled in me values that will leave a legacy and impact generations to come.

They have not done this because of anything that I have done, for I have simply been seeking. These successful people have been more willing to share their wisdom and counsel than I had ever imagined. However, I have made it easy for them to coach me and I have given them the ability to speak into my life, correcting me when I need it and steering me in the right direction. This is something you will need to seek out as well. A mentor is a person who has gone before you, and an example of what you may want to become. They have seen what you will see and done what you want to do. The most important aspect of mentorship is to choose your mentors wisely. It has been said, "Look at your mentor and you will see your future." The people that we listen to, will regardless of intention, steer us in the direction that their lives have gone. The question we must ask ourselves is, "Is that the direction that I want to go?" This one question will determine a tremendous amount about the lives we will live in the future. Who will you seek out, who will you ask for counsel, and who will you choose to learn from?

For the most successful people in the world, mentorship has

been the key factor to their success. I encourage everyone to seek out books from John Maxwell. This man is changing the world by mentoring world leaders on leadership. He has mentored every U.S. President since Ronald Reagan (excluding President Obama.) He educates leaders of the United Nations, recently the President of Argentina, and thousands of others from the greatest corporate leaders to the greatest political icons and even the greatest athletes and sports teams of our time. He teaches that everything rises and falls on leadership. Who is leading you? After leaving the nest of our parents' houses and after leaving the halls of our high schools and universities, it is often our bosses who become our mentors. Ask yourself if your boss or supervisor has the life that you want to live and if they don't, then it is your responsibility to seek out mentors who live the way you want to live. We must find multiple counselors in different areas that we want to excel in.

It is not often that one person will have exact life that you want. So we may need to find different mentors for different parts of our lives. I have found mentors for every walk of life. The physical (fitness), social, emotional, financial, and spiritual areas of my life are all guided by different people. I bounce my ideas and concerns off many mentors and thus am able to find the best suited choice for where I want to go. It has been important to keep from imposing on my coaches and I am sure to make any counsel sessions convenient and easy for them. After all, they have the lives I want, and they are mentoring me out of the goodness of their hearts and to fulfill their desire to find meaning.

It is my responsibility and privilege to gather wisdom from the words they speak. I was told that the greatest leaders are the ones that can turn a crumb into a feast. When listening to these people all it takes is a sentence or two for them to change a life. They have insight that is so deep and rich that mere sentences may bring you closer to their understanding and force growth in ways yet not considered. This is why famous quotes are so popular; one quotation can change many lives. One "crumb" I recently heard is, "Stop the glorification of busy." This forced me to look at my life and analyze the wasted tasks that I fill my life with, all in the hopes of staying busy. It taught me that as a society we may be glorifying a busy life and missing the ideal of an impactful life.

NETWORKING

With technology bringing us closer together, we are able to maintain nearly constant communication. While this provides us a deeper understanding of each others' lives; more communication often means we have less to say. Our exchanges have been shortened, often reduced to common expressions or three letter acronyms. With more frequent communication, we may be losing the art of conversation. Instead of listening, we are often reading what each other is saying off of a screen. Often completely missing the context and nearly always missing the emotions from their voice. Are we losing the skill of listening? When did we leave the days of eloquent expression? It was almost poetic the way our founding fathers spoke to each other and the writing they left behind for us. The intellectual art of conversation was so rich, that although history leaves us with only mere sentences. We gain a richer, deeper understanding of who each person was, what they believed in, and the respect they had for each other. This was at a time when the fastest and easiest communication was often cross country by horse.

The most amazing people in my life are people whom I have gotten to listen tell their stories over coffee or the dinner table. Now I can understand who they are, where they have come from, and what they have achieved. I understand how they feel about their experiences and I feel the emotion that comes out when they are reliving an experience. With Facebook type communication, we get more condensed conversations, less words used, and much of the content left out. This actually leads to less effective communication and less understanding. One of the greatest skills I've learned in this regard is the art of asking questions. What makes interviewers great like Katie Couric, Oprah, or Larry King? What makes their audience want to tune in daily? It is their talent in the art of asking questions. Their guests truly enjoy speaking with them because they have mastered the art of conversation through asking questions. We must learn to appreciate the face to face conversations and we should each be eager to schedule coffee meetings and social lunches. Some of the greatest lessons can come from riding shotgun in a car with your mentors, whether it was hundreds of miles or just around the block. You can ask them questions and receive the quality explanations that come with their undivided attention.

That being said, these networking tools like Facebook and Linked-in can be incredibly effective and beneficial. Linkedin.com has become a fantastic network for employers to research their candidates and follow career changes and availability. With the ability to acquire letters of recommendation from past employers and colleagues, our prospective employers are able to read about our great qualities and skills easily. While seeking employment, it is smart to develop a network of peers, potential employers, and possible mentors. A mentor is usually a person who is excited to share their experience and wisdom with someone who is truly interested in learning. One of the greatest comments ever made to me by a multi-millionaire was how surprised he was that so few people seek his advice and wisdom.

When using these tools, understand that what you post is usually visible to employers and prospective employers. Even when you have your privacy filters on, you can bet that it can be found. There are no secrets on the internet, and many employees and job seekers have been disqualified or terminated based on the pictures and comments that were posted on their Facebook page. The reason being is that you are representing your company when you're at work and even when you are not. Your friends, Facebook friends, and family members know who you work for. If you are showcasing your wild lifestyle publically, be sure that the company you work for is being branded by your behavior. "What type of people work for that company?" is often a question asked by consumers and clients.

This goes back to the principle of stability; do your actions communicate a life of stability that your customers and employer can depend on? Also, be aware of what your friends are posting involving you. Even if you are being careful about how you showcase your life, your friends may not understand this same principle. If I click on photos on your Facebook page, I am able to see pictures that your friends have tagged you in. You will have to decide how you want to handle this possibility. We are in an age where we are all celebrities. Everyone is famous in a small town, and Facebook is a really big "small town."

THE POWER OF ASSOCIATION

The most powerful force in our lives will be our association. Meaning, the people who we spend most of our time with will have the strongest influence in our lives. Your parents may have asked you, "If Jack jumped off of a bridge, would you follow him?" There is an important message in this age old saying. The same question can be asked like this, "If Jack decided to sit on his couch all day, mooch off his folks, and defeat every level of Call of Duty; would you do the same?" Your friends are most likely not going to pay your bills in the future. When your spouse needs a new car or your child needs braces, which of your friends is going to pay for those expenses? If your friends are not going to support you financially then why do they need to support your financial decisions?

It may be time to be the innovator in your group, and decide to redefine your lifestyle to build a great future. If this is the case I encourage you to read the book, The Dream Giver by Bruce Wilkinson. This book is about what a person with a dream will need to go through to achieve their goals, which includes shaking up their sphere of influence a little bit. If you are lucky enough to have a group of friends who are already focused on developing the areas of life we address in this book, then I encourage you to really appreciate your group of friends. I encourage you all to become people that your friends can respect, come to for advice, and emulate as they develop in their careers. Becoming a leader means becoming a person worth following. In business, leaders are the backbones of their companies, and they are heavily sought after.

Allow me to paint you a picture of an experiment done with chimpanzees. Scientists placed one chimpanzee in a large cage with a tall tree in the middle. The tree held bunches of bananas at the top, easily within reach of the master climber. However, when the chimp got to the top of the tree, scientists were there ready to spray the chimp with a water hose. The chimp climbed down dazed, shook off the water, got his bearings and began to climb back up the tree for the bananas. The same result occurred time and time again until the chimp would no longer climb the tree. The scientists put another chimp in the cage with the first and took the water hose away from the tree. The "new" chimp tried to climb the tree, but the defeated tenant who'd already tried and been sprayed, wouldn't allow the new chimp to climb the tree. I have to believe that in chimp language the first chimp was saying, "Oh man don't even try, it can't be done. You will only fail, it's not worth it." One by one the scientists introduced new chimps into the cage and every time the "experienced" tenants would pull the new chimp off the tree. Then, the scientists removed the first chimp from the cage… this was the only chimp to have been actually been sprayed by water. They introduced one final chimp and still the same result occurred, where the new chimp, was pulled from the tree in his attempt to claim to the bananas. What the scientists found is that even though none of the chimps knew what waited for them atop the tree, they wouldn't let anyone else climb to find out.

We cannot be so caught up following the trends, or other people's directions, that we miss out on new experiences or opportunities. Even if someone else had a bad experience doing something similar or even the same thing, we must pursue our goals. Dare to dream, to explore, and to be different. If we don't try then we cannot beat the odds to prove what can be done. Far too many people will offer us their insight and opinions which are given with great intentions, but are usually not completely credible. Their purpose is to keep us from disappointment, but without knowing it, they are also keeping us from success. Reading the book The Dream Give taught me that it is my responsibility to follow my dreams and the only people who told me it wouldn't work were the ones who had given up on their own. It may be a long journey through desolate lands and some depressions, but it will make you stronger and give you satisfaction beyond measure. The success to be found can teach you what you are truly capable of and it will give you loads of confidence in yourself. Believe in yourself and what you can accomplish and you will be incredibly happy that you followed your dreams.

SECTION 3
MECHANICS

BEGINNING THE JOURNEY

Once we have decided upon a goal/desired career, it is time to make the moves and choices that will give us that opportunity. Now, it is vital to remember that there are many paths to any destination and the most important part of the journey is to have a destination established. If we shoot for nothing we will hit it every time. Our dream career may change as we journey toward our goals and we will most certainly run into challenges and obstacles along the way. I hope you find comfort in knowing the journey in itself is an adventure. We will gain experience from every opportunity we take along the way and these lessons, skills, and experiences will provide the next step to get to the opportunities we desire. Regardless of whether we step out of a university program or we are headed straight into our careers, each of us will have to take steps to get to where we want to go. So take on roles that are relevant for your desired job. Then engage in developing the skills that you will need once you get there.

We do what we have to do until we find what we are meant to do.

With job security nearly becoming an oxymoron, it is important to develop skills and continually acquire new ones. There will always be a high demand for efficient, quality work combined with great people skills. The types of people skills that make others feel good about themselves while making it easier for them to accomplish their goals. Regardless of whether a person with these skills gets laid off from a struggling company, they will undoubtedly be picked up by another. These types of people will always be sought after and highly paid. So, to ensure that we are these people, it will be important to gain every bit of experience and insight from any position we hold.

Whether we work as a Cashier at McDonald's or CEO of Starbucks, we should strive to know everything about that business that we can. We must make it our goal to become the best at what we do and gain the necessary skills and understanding to move up the ranks and execute the company strategy. I have learned management skills, managing overhead expenses, and scheduling by working my way up from a Pizza Delivery Boy to a Kitchen Supervisor. I have developed skills in marketing and advertising by working as Marketing Development Director for a major equipment company. I learned how to negotiate a sale and tailor fit deals to clients through selling advertisement to small businesses for news stations across the country. I have learned the ins and outs of finance through being a Personal Banker. I have even learned the risks and requirements involved in starting and operating small businesses. I have been able to utilize my knowledge and experience to assist others in getting great opportunities as a Professional Recruiter.

Every job has prepared me for the next and made me a very qualified candidate for my ultimate goal, which is Venture Capital and Entrepreneurship. Along with social skills I've learned through reading great books and practice and I am no longer concerned about losing my job or finding another. I know that I will always find a place in great companies. I learned the importance of this principle as a Pizza Delivery Boy, where I was always eager to learn a new skill in the pizza parlor. My biggest goal in that company was to become a manager and learn how to work with people to get things accomplished. The idea was to make myself indispensable by learning all I could to move on to the next level of opportunity. My eagerness to develop was noticed and my hard work was rewarded. My next big step was when I moved into the city of Seattle from a small Montana town. I brought a work ethic and my small town love for people with me and that's about it.

When I got a position in marketing development I got my first taste of working with businesses. I loved it and had visions of becoming an advertising mogul, developing major campaigns for billion dollar companies. My desire to learn helped me develop an eye for the media and learn what businesses needed in order to succeed. I learned about brand image and reputation and how that affected market share and revenue. This experience gave me the opportunity to take a position in advertising sales with a major start up partnering with the biggest news networks across the company. I brought my understanding of marketing to thousands of small businesses across the country and was able to tailor fit ad campaigns to their target markets. This experience enabled me to learn about the ins and outs of running a small business in dozens of industries. Through my partnership with these small businesses I was able to learn their financial needs and the many different methods of providing finances for expansion and overhead costs.

When I was ready to move on to the next step I was warmly welcomed into the world of finance. Finance in business has always been a passion for me since I was young boy. My father instilled in me an enthusiasm toward investing and an understanding of risk and return. I am currently, as this is being written, working with families and individuals to educate them and assist them in preparing and providing for their futures. It is a joy to work with these clients, yet I still am eager to learn more and grow. I have my eyes set now on commercial banking and working with business owners to launch, run, and expand their companies. From there I hope to step into the world of venture capital where I will research, understand, and invest in new ideas and innovative projects. It is my goal to be on the forefront of commerce in all that I do and I am excited to be in the middle of where technology and finance converge.

As you may realize, my journey through my career has been a very unorthodox one. I do not have a degree in finance or business, but my experience and real world understanding qualifies me to enter highly competitive and regulated industries. I have learned along the way that most companies, when it comes down to the wire, are eager to select the candidate with applicable experience. This is because that experience of being under pressure, when large profits are at stake, is critical. If you choose to go straight into the work force with the goal of working your way to where you want to be, then understand that there will be different challenges for you. You will have to learn quickly about paying bills, budgeting, and preparing for the future. It may be a longer journey as well, but I believe that you will benefit greatly from your victories and challenges.

For those of us that choose to enter college and work toward our degrees. I would encourage you to gain as much work experience as you can in the summer and any free time you've got. The majority of companies today are still interested in a college degree. It is not the deciding factor by any means and is often irrelevant if a candidate lacks experience in the job market. I have heard many graduates say this, "They won't hire me because I don't have job experience, but how am I going to get job experience if no one will hire me?" If you have a resume that can accompany your diploma, showing your summer work or your summer internship, then a company will feel more comfortable hiring you. This is because they know that you have experienced what it takes to make money and you have the basic understanding of how a company runs from the inside. A job during school can also reduce the debt load the average graduate accrues.

THE SWITCH

Through my journey in the job world I have learned that it is always easier to get a new job when you have a job. This being said a prospective employer will want to know why you are choosing to leave your current position. Be sure to give them a few reasons that you would like to join their company other than higher pay. For me, sometimes it was that I wanted to get into a new industry, others I was ready for new challenges and promotions were not currently available. There are obviously reasons you are interested in leaving or else you would not be leaving, so tell them the truth as long as it is not negative toward your current employer. Nearly all negativity expressed toward your current employer will send up red flags in your interview. Everyone knows there are two sides to a coin, and this will leave them wondering why you have had this experience and what your current company would have to say about the same situation. It is best to showcase your great relationship with your current company while your reason for leaving can be to further pursue your career goals. Good relationships in your current position show that you are able to get along with your co-workers, also that you enjoy building these relationships and working as a team.

Lindsey, a University of Washington Graduate, told me that she did not feel prepared or confident enough to enter the work force after college. She went to work with her father at his company in order to get some experience. She now works in retail at Lu-lu Lemon, and she told me that retail has been a great start for her and has offered her many networking opportunities and valuable experience. She now runs the social media and marketing side of her branch which gives her the opportunity to grow a career in marketing.

Kyler Frisbee

Sitting in Starbucks one day I met a man named Joe. Joe has a drafting degree and shared with me the most important aspects of his journey through his career in drafting. He has worked for many companies and is again in school majoring in physics. He shared with me that the most satisfying part of his experience has been seeing his contributions further the success of each company he has worked for, even long after he left. That feeling is how he knows that he is a quality employee with much to offer. This attitude will ensure that he feels confident and capable to succeed in any role he interviews for in the future.

SHARPENING THE SPEAR

Cover Letter

Just as we addressed the importance of your physical appearance in the beginning of this book, the same principle goes for your resume and cover letter. This is often the very first interaction a hiring manager or recruiter has with you and this will often determine whether they will ever see you in person. So these pieces of paper need to be clean, crisp, easily understood pieces. The cover letter is a chance for the reader to hear your voice and sample the quality of your written communication. If your cover letter is boring or dry, your reader will unintentionally disengage. So it is more important to write the way you would speak than it is to write to the standards of an English class. Indulge in creativity and even humor, because this will stand out. Just be sure that it is tasteful and classic.

I would advise any job seeker to dedicate an extensive amount of time composing a high quality cover letter. This cover letter will be a mission statement communicating what it is you are striving to accomplish? I believe it is much more effective to use one broad cover letter for a large number of applications vs. writing a quick cover letter for every prospective employer. We should approach this task with the same mentality that an author will have when writing his or her next novel. The importance of every word and every sentence should be scrutinized in depth. This is a piece of literature and should be seen as one by all who read it, including the writer. Does the cover letter create an accurate depiction of you and the qualities you would like to portray? Does it have a smooth flow and will it be easy to digest or will your audience be forced to read and re-read multiple times in order to understand the context? If the cover letters are hard to read, they will be tossed without thought.

Resume

Once the style and flair of your greatest professional qualities are shared with your readers they will appreciate a well organized, easy to read resume. One that is crisp and structured and easily read with order and efficiency. It will need to have a system in which the reader can easily see all the vital information without having to search for say, the title of the position you last held or the dates of employment. Each position listed will need to be filled with quality content that is well thought out and planned. We need to put ourselves in the shoes of the reader and ask ourselves, "What information would be most important for me to know about this candidate." Your readers' eyes should not strain to learn why you are a qualified candidate. If you are unable to effectively communicate through a well thought out piece of writing, then how will you be expected to communicate on the fly when the pressure is on? If the cover letter is the soul and spirit of our professional being, then the resume is the skeleton that holds it all together.

A good template for a resume can be found on-line and all that is needed is to fill in the blanks. It is important to give much thought to the words on a resume. These sentences need to be extremely concise and powerful statements. Be sure to list the measurable achievement of each of your prior positions. Such as number of clients helped in an average day, amount of revenue you generated throughout your time there and any recognition received from colleagues, partners, and clients. This assures your reader that you understand what contributions were important to the company. It is also effective to list what skills and lessons were learned in each position, emphasizing those that will be of benefit to you in the particular job you are aiming for.

THE HUNT

Casting Your Net

Once you have constructed a resume and cover letter, it is a great idea to find a recruiting company; preferably one that specializes in your area of interest. It should not be difficult to arrange an appointment with a staffing agency or recruiting company because they get paid by employers when you get hired; if they find you a job. So these resources should be the first that we tap into. Contacting and meeting with multiple recruiters will expand the net that you are casting into the job market. If you have three recruiting companies looking to get you hired, then you will have your pick when they each come back with two or three options. That is with the assumption that you treat these recruiters as if they were the hiring managers for your most desired companies or firms. These people will be your greatest allies if you are able to impress them with your professional appearance and character.

The next benefit these recruiting companies offer, besides joining you on your job hunt, is their experience in building quality resumes. They will take your resume and polish it until it shines. Remember, these people work with you to impress the employers who are looking for you. These people should not be taken for granted because they are the first step in our process of finding the right job. Often times their reputation is placed on the line when they arrange an interview for you and the companies they work with. If we can't impress these recruiters with our determination, focus, and qualifications then we can be sure that they will not be placing us in the best opportunities they have. Think of your first interview with a staffing agency as your first interview with your dream company. First we must impress the recruiters and then we get a chance to impress our prospective employers. Always be sure to write letters, emails, and make phone calls to thank these recruiters after you have met with them. Often this little act of sincerity will imprint on their memory that you are an amazing person, because you may be the only person that week to show your appreciation.

Taking Aim

Once you've gotten one, two, or three recruiting companies assisting you in your job search, it is time to prepare to enter the hunt yourself. Armed with a well polished resume and some guidance from this book, your recruiters, and any other resources you've absorbed; it is time to get to work. Today, there are dozens, maybe even hundreds of websites that take newspaper want ads to a whole new level. Websites like careerbuilder.com, monster.com, and dozens more offer a place for employers to list jobs that they have open. These companies also allow candidates to build profiles with resumes and submit applications to potential employers. A person can search for an hour, find a dozen jobs they're interested in, and apply for them all at the same time. Today, we can do in one hour what would have taken a whole week to do ten years ago.

You may be wondering why a candidate should even search for a job themselves when they have professional recruiters looking for them. Well if you have 75 candidates for a job and you get paid when you find a company the person they hire, are you going to send all 75 or are you going to send the most qualified 3 or 4? It would be ludicrous to expect a company to pay a recruiter to find them the best candidates and then interview 75 people themselves. The reason a company will contract a recruiting company is because they don't have the time to interview, background check, and explain the position and company to 75 different people. So while you do have three recruiters looking for you, they are kind of like the extra fishing pole you leave unattended at the end of the dock in hopes of catching a fish.

Also, recruiting companies often work with big businesses that employ hundreds of people. So their pool of available jobs do not usually include the small businesses and start ups that often offer the best working environments and the greatest potential for career growth. So while your recruiters are searching the main stream, you may find exactly what you were dreaming of in an ad on a website or through word of mouth from a friend.

INTERVIEWING

Prior to attending an interview, be sure to research the company you will be meeting with. It is important that you are up to speed with at least the surface image of the company you'd like to work for. Little facts that you find may seem unimportant, but by telling an interviewer that you know their company was founded in x year and they did x amount of dollars in sales last year; they will know that you are truly interested in their company and that you are able to do independent research. Again this may not get you the job, but it will set you apart from many of the candidates. That is the goal of our process. To separate ourselves from our competition every chance we get!

When the conversation begins, be sure to go slow. The interviewer will dictate the flow and direction of the conversation and it is important to keep your composure. The speed at which you answer questions will communicate the way that you prefer to communicate. When a person slows down in conversation it symbolizes intent in word choice and message. It shows confidence, while allowing you to be more comfortable and stable in your answers. We need to sit up tall and be aware of our body language. We must feel comfortable making ourselves seen by lifting our heads, broadening our shoulders, and using our hands to communicate also. Our nonverbal communication is key and without knowing it we are communicating what we really think about ourselves. This is why the previous chapters in this book are so vital. The chapters we have gone through, hopefully, have helped us to build a stronger self-image and grow our confidence.

Now it was brought to my attention by a colleague that handshakes say very much about a person. There are two extreme ends of the handshake spectrum. Each extreme will show lack of confidence and belief in self. A limp handshake makes people feel like the other person is barely holding on. It is almost like someone needs to muster all the courage they have in order to put their hand in yours. Now an overbearing hand-crushing handshake communicates that a person is either overcompensating for their low self-image, or they feel like they are the most powerful person in the world and they want you to know it too. Both extremes are quick ways to begin an interview on the wrong foot. The premium handshake is palm to palm, where the base of both thumbs meet, clasping the hand and giving it a secure squeeze that says, "I'm happy to meet you…This is going to go well."

Now, what do we say in order to make the best impression? The answer to that question is also a balancing point between two ideals. The first is that we need to carry ourselves in a way that communicates that this interview is not our only opportunity. We do not need to say this, but it is important to remember this principle. The interview you are in is not the only interview available to you. The best way to prepare for an interview is to book another with another company. The more appointments you have lined up; the more confidence you will develop in the process. Do not be afraid to fail in an interview, Thomas Watts said, "If you double your rate of failure, you will double your rate of success." The idea is that as long as you are taking a swing at the ball you have the chance to hit it. No one has ever hit a home run without swinging the bat. Regardless of a good interview or bad, tell yourself, "Today I did well; tomorrow I'll do better."

Employers, just like single guys and gals, do not want a person who is desperate. Let's say my friend is a single guy and he is interested in meeting the right woman. Now let's say I meet a great woman that would be perfect for my friend. If I tell my friend, " I just met this amazing gal who would be perfect for you. She will date anyone," do you think he will be excited to meet her? I don't think so. Most employers want a person who has options; because this means that other people see them as quality people who have a great deal to offer. Along with knowing that you are a desired candidate, a company also wants to know why you want to work with them. The mentality is that, "I have several interviews and other opportunities available to me, but I want to work here, because…." This is when our reasons for choosing this company will come into play. We must not be afraid to express our genuine desire to join the company we choose. This desire does not show desperation, it shows intent and foresight.

A great sentence to use to communicate this is, "I have a few opportunities that have been presented to me and I am looking into them. However, I really want to work with you because I believe in your company, the way you do business, and the vision you have for the future." This comment should not be fluff or a bluff. When you are scheduling interviews be sure to tell this to the company that you really want to work for, maybe even the top three. By expressing your desire to work with them, you show that you have thought this through, developed a plan, and committed yourself to making it happen.

It is important to remember that manners go a long way. A simple gesture like arriving early ensures that your interviewing counterpart will be able to swiftly move into your appointment regardless of what they were doing before or have to do next. This communicates, again, that their time is important to you. If you show this respect to your future employer, they will believe that you will show the same respect to their customers. Sending a thank you card, email, or phone call to whomever interviews you will also set you apart from the rest in their eyes, just like it did with the recruiters. Be sure your message is more than just a thank you. Now, go a bit further by telling them about your excitement and gratitude, and that while you are meeting other companies; you are hoping to hear back from them.

Great Candidates are in High Demand

Now that you have the job, remember that you are more important to your company than you will ever imagine. You and your colleagues are the heart, soul, and skin of the company. Without you there is no company. So remember that you are not some expendable piece of equipment unless you see yourself as such. Do great work to make yourself known, and show others your great character and superb skills. Remind them time and time again why you were hired and what you are capable of accomplishing. This book is meant to connect the needs and expectations of employers with a group of people who are interested in meeting and exceeding these same expectations. The baby boomers and their children have families. Most of them are grandparents, and these same business owners, executives, and so forth are retiring more and more every year. With the next generation focused on having families while their parents are retiring. It is time to step into these significant roles as major contributors. We will be more and more vital to these companies who are looking for qualified candidates both academically and socially. Never sell yourself short thinking that you are just a number on an employee list. You are what you make yourself and if you want to be a CEO, Executive, or anything else. It is up to you to make it happen and you absolutely can!

SECTION 4
WHAT IS NEXT

FINANCIAL SECURITY

With the income that we are now creating, it is vital to consider the next phase of life. What treasures are we saving to ensure that our retirement years are golden? In regards to financial stability and prosperity I believe that for the large majority of us, a job is the best foundation. A foundation that will ensure that we can keep food on our tables, clothes on our backs, and roofs over our heads...for now. Each of us needs to begin to think about whether or not we ever want to retire from our jobs. Are we content with a plan that has us working until we die? How much do we understand about what it takes to retire? How will we provide for ourselves and our loved ones if we do retire? A common misconception about retirement is that no matter our choices we all get to retire at 65 and social security will provide for us. There are many factors that go into that myth, but the truth is that retirement is based on net wealth and residual income...not age.

With thousands of ventures "promising" fantastic returns it is hard to know for sure what will pay off. Through much training I have come to understand the most common avenues for financial planning. The stock markets have been a very popular sector for retirement planning with company matched 401k's and IRA's. Many people have chosen to invest independently in the market with the service of stock brokers. The real estate market has been a very popular sector as well, where individuals and couples purchase a home or apartment complex and rent out the housing, using the rental income to pay off the mortgage and supplement their lifestyle. This is usually done with the hope that by the time the mortgage is paid off; they will be able to live completely off of their rental income or sell the house and attain the money that the renters paid.

Many people have used their paychecks to invest in small businesses with the hopes that their business will provide financial stability and options in their retirement. There are thousands of other ways to provide for your golden years, but the importance of understanding our options and building a plan is crucial. Each of these common vehicles of financial security has risk and reward. It is vital that we do not follow blindly what the common masses are doing and we be determined to understand our options.

Currently the Social Security Administration has reported that 98.3% of people are either dead or broke at the age of 65. The term broke meaning that their lifestyles are being supplemented by family, charity, or government aid. The SSA reports that all that is required to be categorized in the 1.7% is a residual income of $3,000 a month. They have also stated that Social Security benefits are not meant to be the sole form of income for any individual. If we are going to be a generation that builds up our global economy for future generations then we must make plans and decisions that will ensure that we are not a part of the 98.3%.

EDUCATION AND RESOURCES

I believe that reading opens up a world of understanding, allowing you to appreciate the great qualities that you already have.

Study business trends and learn about the industries that you are interested in. You can broaden your horizon by learning more about different markets and industries. Through this research you will find what drives and industry and what you didn't expect to be involved. You can also find out how different industries connect and where our economy has been. Along the way I encourage you to research who founded this country. What principles did they use to establish this great nation? How can we honor the men and women who have given their lives to allow us to do what we choose? All of this can be found on the internet, in the library, and in the memories of many around us.

I encourage each of us to learn about our international affairs, as well as our import and export business and regulations. Many jobs are being outsourced to foreign countries due to the financial advantages and the fact that India and China are graduating more English speaking individuals than America. Pay attention to this and learn which industries will be affected by these changes. As the world economies grow closer together; innovation becomes more abundant and our ability to stay up to date with these changes that becomes more vital.

What started as a way to share memories between friends has become the second largest search engine in the world. It is now the largest classroom that has ever existed and, currently, provides humanity with over 80 million hours of video a day. It is predicted that more than 90% of the webs content will be video in the near future. Now if you are not sure how to choose a suit or if you need help tying your tie, your answer and teacher are only a few key strokes away. Whether you want to learn how to do the latest dance or you need help with your geometry; your answer is on Youtube.com. I have spent hundreds, maybe thousands of hours listening to people like Warren Buffet talk about how they built their fortunes. I've listened to Will Smith talk about what it takes to be successful. I have learned that I am a Champion and that even the most unlikely people can be the next big thing. Take this technology and utilize it for your empowerment in all areas of your life. I have seen the best videos on marriage counseling, leadership principles, and what to expect from upcoming years in technology. It allows me to stay current with what is important to people around the world and connect with people who share my same interests. With the greatest classroom of all time, full of teachers who are doing what we want to do, we are in an age when everything truly is possible. Do you want to change your stripes and become financially successful? Take a seat and listen to people like Robert Kiyosaki, Bill Gates, Warren Buffet, Donald Trump, and Dave Ramsey. Anything you want to be, you can find the mentors on Youtube.com.

Coursera.com is a company/website that partners with the top universities around the world to provide millions of people with free college education. Their vision is to provide world class education to people who never would have had the chance. Whether you are interested in finance, economy, media, technology, or whatever you choose; there is a class for you. You will be provided with online courses that do not require traditional time commitments and the best part is that when the course is completed, each participant will receive a certificate of their completion. Perhaps you want to pursue a career in finance, you can show your future employer your certificate of completion for the intro to finance course from Stanford University. Many accredited universities will accept these certificates for credits. Think of getting part of your education from ivy-league schools for free. Take a look and see what Coursera.com has to offer you. It's your life, your education, without your checkbook.

Are you interested in the newest breakthroughs in the medical field, tech field, or social sciences? If you are then you will love

Ted.com, Ideas Worth Spreading. International businessmen and women are historically respected for their understanding of many industries. Take a moment to learn what a PHD in Literature learned in her year spent homeless. Take a glimpse into the groundbreaking research that is providing insight into social trends and innovations in space and material sharing. Ted.com brings together some of the most dynamic and fascinating people of our time, each giving talks about what they are dedicating their lives to. These talks are truly inspiring, motivational, and encouraging causes that will make the world a better, more understood place than it has ever been before. Imagine going to a conference where Jesus, Gandhi, Abraham Lincoln, Winston Churchill, Mother Teresa and the rest of the most impactful men and women of time have gathered together to each give a talk about what they were passionate about. Ted.com brings together all of the game changers in the present time, our time. So I encourage you to go further than the average, learn more than most care to know, and support causes that will impact generations to come.

One of the greatest forms of continued education for me has been found in books like: How to Win Friends by Dale Carnegie, Win by Frank Luntz, Magic of Thinking Big by David J. Schwartz, The Richest man in Babylon by George S. Clason, The Dream Giver by Bruce Wilkinson, and there are hundreds more that I have read. I have to thank these authors for putting into writing the amazing lessons that they have learned over their lifetimes. Through these books their wisdom will be passed down for generations to come.

This book has been about the business and career aspects of life. I am a believer of a well rounded life and continually explore the arts and the spiritual journey of humanity. I am a believer in Christ and must thank God for the blessings in my life. I believe that much of my inner piece comes from my belief and lessons I have learned about transcendence from the Book the Power of Now by Eckhart Tolle.

I would like to thank everyone who contributed to this book. I'd like to thank my amazing mentors, friends, and family. As well as the people who offered their experiences and advice in passing. Often strangers, who I could only speak with for a brief moment, each of whom impacted me in a special way.

I believe that we are all made for greatness and our journeys to fulfill our potential will be rewarding in themselves. I hope that this information is helpful in setting each of us up for success in our careers and financial futures. I hope that we will all understand money and the difference we can make in the world by being responsible in regards to how we get it and what we do with it. I am a member of the NINJA generation...New Industries New Jobs New Abilities!!! Go and Grow!

ABOUT THE AUTHOR

My name is Kyler Frisbee and I was born in Seoul, South Korea. At 9 months old I was adopted and from there I was raised in Montana; a place that was once the Wild West…a lawless country. It was a place that gold prospectors rested, with their guns close by, on their way to the Gold Rush in California. It is a majestic place known for its mountain grandeur, beautiful lakes, and welcoming people. It is known as the last best place on Earth aka the Big Sky Country. My childhood was one that dreams are made of…until I got to middle school and realized that I was part of a shockingly small population of Asians. I was one of three students who came from Asian descent in my high school. This was a blessing in disguise, because I learned how to be an independent thinker and a person who was not afraid of what others said about me. I developed a thick skin and learned that prejudice, discrimination, and even racism are simply symptoms of misunderstandings. My family has been incredible in their support throughout my youth and early adulthood. I learned more than I realized…a huge part of that was how to succeed in business.

From as long as I can recall, I've looked up to the business man in his suit and tie. I can remember thinking a briefcase was the ultimate symbol of success. It's funny that deep down all I wanted to become was a business man. However, in high school I chose a completely opposite route and I got extremely involved in snowboarding. With my father's help and my families support I was able to experience incredible opportunities on the snow. Some of my photos have been used in advertisements by Alaskan Airlines, Patagonia, and my home mountain in Whitefish, MT. These photos are memories of my incredible childhood and the challenges I overcame in my pursuit of greatness.

Meanwhile my family continued their pursuit of excellence in the business world. My father opened 3 financial advisory offices in Montana for some of the largest financial institutions in America. He is also one of the greatest skiers to make a turn and the biggest reason for my success on the snow. My older brother currently works as a Senior VP for a trust company managing over 4 billion dollars in assets. His wife became a brand specialist for one of America's oldest companies after she met my brother at Vanderbilt University where they both finished their graduate degrees in business. My sister currently works in the world renowned software and computing company, Microsoft; as a Solutions Manager for their recruiting software. Her husband worked his way through College after emigrating from Guatemala. After he graduated with his bachelors he went on to graduate from Harvard Business with his MBA and currently works as Chief Financial Officer for a very successful company headquartered in Mukilteo, WA. My younger brother has been working on his journeymen's license since he was nearly 21. Now at 24 he is an amazing young father and he has a great future ahead of him. I know that he will do great things with the immense amount of integrity and talent he has. His example has actually been one of the biggest inspirations for me to pursue a productive career. My mother has been one of the most successful people I know in raising four amazing children. She taught me compassion and acceptance of others through her great work in family planning and home healthcare. She and my father adopted me and my younger brother. They have managed to raise children who absolutely love their parents and enjoy any time they get to spend together. Our family would not be complete without a single person who I've mentioned.

I have been raised with a keen eye for what works in business and professional relationships. Subconsciously I have been programmed for success and I have been given skills and insight that I did not realize I had. I was 18 years old when I headed to college for no reason at all, unsure of what I could contribute to society. I was lost and confused and my only hint for the future was my love of business and my love for people. So from there I began my journey, back to school with no direction at all. Until one day I went to hear a young man speak who I had met years back. By building an E-commerce business he had become very successful at a young age. He had just moved to Seattle, WA to deepen his relationships with 3 of the most successful men either of us had ever met, whose annual combined income totaled over 14 million dollars. He introduced me to his mentors and business partners, who took me under their wings.

It was my gut feeling that made me follow suit and after a 16 hour journey to Portland, OR and then on to Seattle, WA; I had made the Puget Sound area my new home. From that day to now I have spent thousands of hours documenting and recording the advice and wisdom of not only these same multi-millionaires, but dozens of other successful entrepreneurs and corporate executives. The contents of this book have been in my head for nearly a decade, but this information is timeless. What it takes to succeed hasn't ever changed; it's just the arena that is always changing. They've taught me what it takes to be successful in business, how to handle finances intelligently, and what other great families look like. I am incredibly grateful for the opportunities that my family, friends, and mentors have provided for me and the wisdom they have all shared.